M000233368

Dear Cecillia & Pascal,

Hope you enjoy these funny stories & illustrations as much as I did growing up. We can't wait to meet you two.

♡ Uncle Wilton &
Auntie Yackie

MAX AND MORITZ
and other
Bad-Boy Stories
and Tricks

Max and Moritz

and other
BAD-BOY STORIES
AND TRICKS

by

Wilhelm Busch

Translated from the German by
Andy Gaus

JAMES A. ROCK & COMPANY, PUBLISHERS
ROCKVILLE • MARYLAND

MAX AND MORITZ
And Other Bad-Boy Stories and Tricks
by Wilhelm Busch
Translated from the German by Andy Gaus

Copyright © 2003 by Andy Gaus
Copyright © 2003 by James A. Rock &. Co., Publishers.

First Edition: August 2003

All applicable copyrights and other rights reserved worldwide.

ALL RIGHTS RESERVED. NO PART OF THIS BOOK MAY BE REPRODUCED
IN ANY FORM OR BY ANY ELECTRONIC OR MECHANICAL MEANS
INCLUDING INFORMATION STORAGE AND RETRIEVAL SYSTEMS
WITHOUT PERMISSION IN WRITING FROM THE PUBLISHERS, EXCEPT
BY A REVIEWER WHO MAY QUOTE BRIEF PASSAGES IN A REVIEW.

Cover Design by Lynne Rock

Special thanks to Lilda RockWiley for her assistance in this project.

Special thanks to A. S. Wensinger for critical guidance.

Address comments and inquiries to:

JAMES A. ROCK & COMPANY, PUBLISHERS
9710 Traville Gateway Drive, #305
Rockville, MD 20850

E-mail:
jrock@rockpublishing.com   lrock@senseofwonderpress.com
Internet URL: www.RockPublishing.com

Paperbound ISBN: 0-918736-17-x
Hardbound ISBN: 0-918736-18-8

Printed in the United States of America

Table of Contents

Detail from the "Trinity Apocalypse," an illuminated manuscript produced in England but written in French. Based on the Book of Revelation, it is dated c. 1250.

Introduction
Max and Moritz
and the Birth of the Funnies

Where do comic strips come from?

That depends on what you mean by "comic strips."

A sequence of pictures to tell a story? Then comics come from French cave paintings, from Egyptian papyruses, and to cut a long list short, from the dawn of time and everywhere.

Humorous pictures using animals as people? Then once again, comics are at least as old as ancient Egypt, where you can find tomb paintings showing, for instance, a mouse dressed in the height of fashion putting on her makeup at her dressing table.

Pictures using dialog balloons? That would include medieval paintings dating from at least as early as 1250.

Mass reproduction of humorous drawings for public distribution? Political and satirical cartoons in the form of woodcuts were a hot item on the streets of European cities in the 14th and 15th centuries.

Are we getting close to Donald Duck yet? Maybe not. For one thing, the full possibilities of picture books really only blossom with the improved printing techniques of the 1800s. And as for printing in color, that is notoriously tricky even today. As late as the 1890s it was still so hellishly tricky that newspaper publishers who acquired the new color printing presses soon abandoned their plans to reproduce great works of art and started printing comics instead because that was the only thing they could print that wouldn't look like a failure.

So what then is the first comic book? Is it Rodolphe Töpffer's *Histoire de Monsieur Jabot,* a satirical picture-book from Switzerland in 1833? Perhaps, but both the detailed drawings and the wordy captions in Töpffer's work are more in the style of old engravings like the political broadsheets already mentioned: they don't have the stripped-down quality of comic-strip art and comic-strip dialogue.

A sample page from Rodolphe Töpffer's Histoire de Monsieur Jabot
(1833), a satirical picture-book from Switzerland.

Is it Heinrich Hoffmann's *Der Struwwelpeter,* known in English as *Slovenly Peter,* certainly an enduring classic in its own right since 1845?

Perhaps, but the work most often mentioned as Comic Book Number One is the one you are holding: Wilhelm Busch's *Max and Moritz,* finally published in Munich in 1865 (after Busch first offered the work for free to a publisher in Dresden who rejected it as not worth the price). And it fully deserves that title: comic books are, finally, not a set of techniques but an experience, and *Max and Moritz* is the first work that unmistakably looks and feels like a comic book.

Two things make that so. One is the drawing style, fluid and with few strokes, engaging your imagination by the fine detail that is not shown as well as by the exaggerated features that are brought to the fore. It amounts to a new form of pictorial plain speech: pictures that seem to speak directly to you in a single clearly understood voice. (By comparison, the elaborate old woodcuts and engravings are more like a choir: the sound is impressive, but it's often hard to make out the words.) And all the fluidity, simplicity, freedom, sharpness of caricature and directness of the comic-book drawing style is fully present in *Max and Moritz* to an extent that has never been surpassed.

But what really gives *Max and Moritz* the feeling of a comic book is having true comic-book characters: Max and Moritz themselves. You see the contrast sharply when you look at *Slovenly Peter.* There a succession of hapless characters passes before your eyes, but no one character stands out, and as a result you only observe the characters, you do not identify with them.

Everybody identifies with Max and Moritz. That is startling, since both the things they do and the things that are done to them are so gruesomely violent that they're only acceptable as happening to cartoon characters (including cartoon animals). Yet you would have to be a very mild and pious person indeed to read *Max and Moritz* and not immediately feel that both of them are you, and that they're doing everything you've always wanted, and that if it leads to an early death, that's a small price to pay. In the 1990s, pop psychologist John

From Heinrich Hoffmann's Der Struwwelpeter, 1845.

Bradshaw made it fashionable for people to talk about their "Inner Child." One gathers that this Inner Child is a well-meaning but put-upon little person something like Heidi. But Bradshaw was 125 years too late: in 1865 Wilhelm Busch revealed, once and for all, the Inner Child within each of us, and it's not Heidi, it's Max and Moritz. And the proof is that no bad child, inner or outer, who gets to know Max and Moritz ever forgets them.

William Randolph Hearst certainly didn't. He encountered Max and Moritz during his boyhood travels in Europe, and when he wanted a sure-fire comic feature for his *New York Journal* in 1897, he told Rudolph Dirks to create "something like Max and Moritz." (Dirks was the son of a German immigrant and needed no explanation.)

The result was *The Katzenjammer Kids*, featuring two mischievous young boys and something Max and Moritz never seem to have had, a mother. A boarder named the Captain and a bearded truant officer named the Inspector were added a few years later.

The Katzenjammer Kids was the first comic strip that made a regular practice of having several panels in sequence and using balloons for all the dialog, so it was the first comic strip that would fit everyone's definition.

History has apparently not recorded Wilhelm Busch's reaction to the Katzenjammer Kids (though he lived till 1908 and surely must have heard about them). Perhaps Busch, who once published an essay about his belief in reincarnation, would have understood how two young boys murdered in an undisclosed German village in the 1860s could have been born again as Hans and Fritz in New York City a generation later.

The cycle of death and rebirth didn't end there. In fact the Katzenjammer Kids split like an amoeba into two strips with identical characters, *The Katzenjammer Kids* and *The Captain and the Kids,* one drawn by the original artist for another paper, and one drawn by another artist for the original paper. There were also a number of rather obvious imitators—also featuring two boys, their momma, a sea captain and his bearded sidekick.

As this book goes to press, more than a hundred years after the first appearance of *The Katzenjammer Kids,* the strip still appears, now drawn by Hy Eisman, in a dwindling number of papers.

But the souls of Max and Moritz have continued to reincarnate, more recently on television as Beavis and Butthead, characters that have been described as edgy and modern (because of their violence? because of their cruelty to animals?) but which really offer nothing not found in *Max and Moritz.* And Max and Moritz are much more shocking because everyone falls in love with them, evil though they are. (Beavis and Butthead are not so shocking that way: not everyone falls in love.)

Actually, Max and Moritz aren't *entirely* bad. *Max and Moritz* isn't just about hurting people, it's also about having the best possible fun and sharing it with your best friend. There is love there, love between two friends who are inseparable till death. Their love just doesn't extend very far into the world beyond them. But many people who love are like that.

One way or another, *Max and Moritz* is such a delightful piece of good fun that it is not surprising that wherever German is spoken, Max and  Moritz are known to all the bad children between the ages of four and 120. What's more surprising is that despite the many translations—at least 13 before this one— Max and Moritz are not known to all the bad children who speak English. Let's do something about that.

Andy Gaus
Boston, April 2003

Wilhelm Busch

Max and Moritz

A BAD-BOY STORY
IN
SEVEN TRICKS

PROLOGUE

Oh dear! We read and hear sometimes
Of nothing else but children's crimes,
Crimes of children such as these:
Max and *Moritz*, if you please!

Wisely though they were instructed
How one's life is best conducted,
They would scorn this tutelary,
Laugh, and secretly make merry.
Ah, when mischief's to be done,
You can count on everyone!
Beast-tormenting, people-grieving,
Pear- and plum- and apple-thieving
Is more comfortable and pleasant,
Naturally, than being present
In the church or in the school,
Sitting tight upon your stool.
But alas, alas, alas,
Seeing what shall come to pass!
Oh, it's sorry to relate
Moritz's and Max's fate!
Here their story lingers on,
Sweetly told and neatly drawn.

TRICK THE FIRST

Many folks are hardy toilers
In the raising of their broilers,
Firstly, for the eggs that they
Can be counted on to lay;
Secondly, since now and then
You can have a roasted hen;
Third, for feathers to upholster
Pillow, cushion, couch, and bolster:
When you lie and rest your head,
No one likes a drafty bed.

Widow Bolt disliked that too.
Look: I've sketched her here for you.

Three fat hens made up her flock,
Guarded by a pompous cock.
Max and Moritz, full of cheer,
Thought, "What good can we do here?"
One, two, three, full steam ahead,
They cut up a loaf of bread
In four pieces, each a stick
Thick as a person's thumb is thick.

These on crossing strings they bind
With a piece at every end.
In Widow Bolt's back yard, with care
They set them down and leave them there.

The rooster sees, and starts to crow
To all the hens, to let them know.
Keekary-kee! Keekary-kee!
Tock, tock, tock—and they all come see.

Hens and rooster swallow gaily
Each a piece into its belly.

But now they see they are not able
To say "Excuse me" and leave the table.

To the south and to the north,
See them tearing back and forth.

Up to the sky! Oh what commotion!
Oh my land! My land o' goshen!

Caught in a branch, they come to rest,
There to make their final nest.
And their necks get stretched and stretcheder,
And their cries get wretched and wretcheder.

After each lays one egg more,
Death comes knocking at the door.

Widow Bolt in her boudoir
Heard the racket from afar;

Out she ambles, full of care;
Oh, what horror met her there!

"Flood my eyes, you tears so burning:
All my hoping, all my yearning,
All my dreams of things to be
Dangle from this apple-tree!"

Deeply moved and sorrow-stricken,
With her knife she cuts each chicken
From the rope that did the strangling,
So they won't just stay there dangling.

With a face as hard as stone,
She returns inside alone.

Trick the first you just have read;
Trick the second lies ahead.

TRICK THE SECOND

When the goodly Widow Bolt
Recovered from her awful jolt,
Thinking back and forth, she guessed
That it really would be best
For those who from this vale of tears
Parted in their tender years,
All in silence, all in gloom
To take them, roast them, and consume.
Granted that the grief was great,
Seeing them in this naked state
On the hearthstone, spread with flour,
They that in a kinder hour
Used so merrily to scratch
In the yard or garden patch.

Widow Bolt must cry anew;
Spitz, her dog, is saddened, too.

Max and Moritz smelled it greedily;
"On the roof," they cried—"and speedily!"

Through the chimney, with desire
They see the hens upon the fire,
Minus head and minus gullet,
Roasting sweetly in the skillet.

Widow Bolt decides to go
To the storage rooms below,

So that from the sauerkraut
She can serve a portion out,
Which especially suits her style
When it has warmed up a while.

Meanwhile, Max and Moritz lurk
Upon the roof and do their work.
Max has brought a rod and line,
Which fit in with his design.

Shnoopdivoop! From off the fire
One has now been taken higher.

Shnoopdivoop! the second hen;
Thirdly, shnoopdivoop again.
Finally, here comes number four;
Shnoopdivoop! Ah, there you are!
Spitz saw everything and now
Barks out loud: Ravow! Ravow!

But already, full of mirth,
They've left the roof and traveled forth.

Widow Bolt comes from below;
Now we'll have a pretty show.
To the floor she stands there rooted,
When she sees her skillet looted.

All the hens were flown away—
"Spitz!!" was all that she could say.

"Spitz, you monster, worst of curs,
Just wait there, and you'll get yours!"

With her heavy spoon of wood,
She works over Spitz but good.
Spitz cries out in injured shame,
As if to say he's not to blame.

Max and Moritz, well concealed,
Lie a-snoring in the field,
And of all the chicken-fest
Just a leg sees light at best.

Trick the second you have read.
Trick the third is just ahead.

TRICK THE THIRD

All the townsmen called by name
A tailor known as Master Swaim.

Coats for Mondays, coats for Sundays,
Shirts and pants and socks and undies,
Vests with pockets for your thumbs,
Parkas, when the winter comes—
All these articles of wearing
Swaim was expert in preparing.
Or if there was fluting, lacing,
Off-removing, on-replacing,
Just a button on your cuff
Either loose or halfway off,
When, wherever, how, or if,
Front or back, it made no diff-
Erence at all to Master Swaim;
Service was his lifelong aim.
Thus, in town from end to end,
All considered him a friend.
But Max and Moritz's reaction
Was to drive him to distraction.

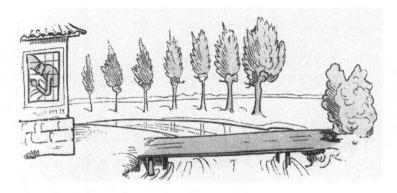

By the Master Tailor's dwelling
Flowed a creek with snarls and swelling,
Plus a simple bridge that spanned
The interval from land to land.

Max and Moritz, never shirking,
Have the saw and now are working:
Scritch! Scratch! Within a minute
They've sawed a little crevice in it.

Once they've put this labor by,
Suddenly one hears the cry:
"Tailor, tailor, I declare:
Stick your needle you know where!"

Swaim could bear the greatest burden
And would never put a word in;
But for once, this really shook him,
And his kindliness forsook him.

Quick he leaves his house of brick
With a stick both long and thick.
And just as he goes to check
He hears a sound like "meck meck meck!"

He's halfway to the other shore;
Crack! The bridge will stand no more.

He hears again that "Meck meck meck!"
Ploom! The water hits his neck.

Just as his demise seems nigh,
Two fat geese come swimming by.
Master Swaim, at end of rope,
Grips them with a grasping grope.

Both the geese caught well in hand,
Thus he flies to drier land.

With this sort of thing, the trouble
Is, that it's not comfortable.

Swaim, for instance, got some crummy
Stomach cramps inside his tummy.

Let Mrs. Swaim be praised in Zion!
For her heated clothing-iron
Brought to health the clammy frame
Of the dripping Master Swaim.

Soon again, throughout the town,
"Swaim is well!" went up and down.

Trick the third you just have read;
Trick the fourth is just ahead.

TRICK THE FOURTH

All the axioms concerning
What one needs by way of learning
Say that not just A-B-C
Makes a man what man should be;
Not just writing, not just reading
Makes for good existence-leading;
Nor should one confine one's action
To addition or subtraction:
These are but cinders in your eyes,
If you are not also wise.

Wisdom is the object sought.
Wisdom's what Pastor Lampel taught.

Max and Moritz, you can guess,
Hardly could have liked him less:
He who spends his time at pranks
Gives a teacher little thanks.

Now this good man of whom I spoke
Owned a pipe and liked to smoke—
Which beyond the slightest bicker,
In an old and pious vicar
After a day of working wearily,
We cannot judge too severely.

Max and Moritz, all unblinking,
Now about that pipe are thinking,
Wondering if, by means of *that*,
This man can't be gotten at.

Sunday soon came round again;
Pastor Lampel, best of men,
In the church with great emotion
Played the organ at devotion.

Max and Moritz, bent on arson,
Softly snuck into the parson's,
Where the Meerschaum pipe would stand;
Max, he holds it in his hand

While Moritz opens up a tin
Of gunpowder and dumps it in.
In a hurry, stuff, stuff, stuff,
They fill the pipebowl full enough.
Quietly, quickly, now to get out:
Any minute church will let out!

Meanwhile, with a tranquil mind,
Lampel leaves his church behind.

And with ledger-books and lists of
Things a pastor's work consists of,
Joyfully he turns his pace
To his ancestral dwelling-place,

And free from every care and gripe,
Kindles his beloved pipe.

"The greatest joy from heaven sent
Is"—he says—"to be content!"

Vroom! There goes the pipe and powder,
Loud as anything and louder.
Coffeepot and coffeetable,
Jug and glass, there's nothing stable;
Stove and chair, there's nothing fast;
All goes flying in the blast.

Soon the smoke begins to rise,
And we see with grateful eyes
That Lampel is alive and kicking,
Though he's taken quite a licking
.

Hands and ears and facial pores are
Just as black as those of Moors are,
And the last remains of hair
Are singed away beyond repair.

Who should work for the promotion,
Now, of learning and devotion?
Who can take his duties over
So that Lampel can recover?
Since the boys have had their joke with
Lampel's pipe, what can he smoke with?

Finally every fracture knits,
Just the pipe remains in bits.

Trick the fourth you just have read.
Trick the fifth is just ahead.

TRICK THE FIFTH

Who in city or in town
Has an uncle settled down
Should be civil and self-possessed:
That's what uncles like the best.
Mornings, say "Good morning to you!
Are there favors we can do you?"
Bring him all he wants to use:
Slippers, pipe and Daily News.
Or if somewhere in his back
It should itch or twitch or crack,
You should be a quick, observant,
Eager, and efficient servant.
If a pinch of snuff or two
Brings from him a harsh Ahchoo,
Express the wish, in flowery terms,
That his renown may spread like germs.
If he comes home late one night,
Tired and maybe slightly tight,
Fetch his cap and robe, with tapers
To guide him through the nightly vapors.
In short, one thinks of all the ways
To brighten up one's uncle's days.

Max and Moritz, for their part,
Found here little to warm their heart.
Just think, the way they set their wits
To plans for ruining Uncle Fritz!

Beetles, as you all have heard,
Though they really aren't a bird,
In the branches, to and fro,
Creeping, crawling, round they go.

Max and Moritz, ever gleeful,
Shake the trunk and catch a treeful.

They stow every tiny creeper
Into a little bag of paper.

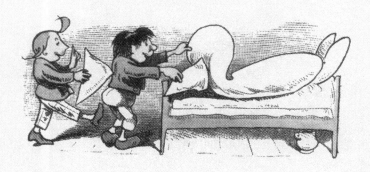

Then for Uncle's bedroom heading,
They unload them in his bedding!

Uncle Fritz goes off to bed,
Pointy cap upon his head;

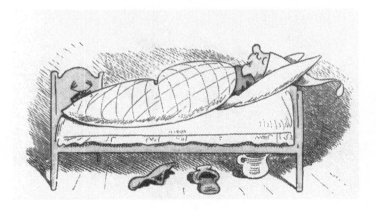

Peacefully his eyes he closes,
Wraps himself up well, and dozes.

Just as he drops off to sleep,
Look, they're coming, creep, creep, creep!

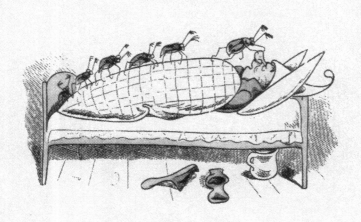

Now the one who's leading those
Grabs at Uncle Fritz's nose.

"Eek, what's that?" he hollers—"Ugh!"
Grasping at the dreadful bug.

Here is Uncle, full of dread,
Whizzing headlong out of bed.

"Ouch!"—he's got one here and there,
Down his legs and through his hair.

On the table, on the wall,
Beetles buzz and fly and crawl.

Terror-stricken, Uncle Fritz
Hacks and tramples them to bits.

Look you well now, that's enough:
No more creepy-crawly stuff!

Uncle Fritz is now composed,
And again his eyes are closed.

Trick the fifth you just have read;
Trick the sixth is just ahead.

TRICK THE SIXTH

In the lovely days of Easter,
When the pious bakermaster
Works with diligence to make
Every sort of sugar cake,
Max and Moritz wished that they
Might share the sweetness of the day.

But the baker, thinking brightly,
Went and locked the bakehouse tightly.

Therefore he who wants to loot
Must employ the chimney route.

43

Rotch! And here they come, dear souls,
Through the chimney, black as coals.

Poof! They fall into the chest
Where the flour is laid to rest.

There! Now like two ghosts they walk,
Round about as white as chalk.

Now the boys address themselves
To the pretzels on the shelves.

Crack! The chairback splinters off;

Shvopp! They fall into the trough.

Covered all around in dough,
Here they make a sad tableau.

Ha! The bakerman discovers
Both the little sugar-lovers.

One, two, three—before you know,
He has rolled two loaves of dough.

In the oven it's still glowing—
Ruff!—so that's where you are going!

Ruff! And here's the finished pasty,
Golden brown and no doubt tasty.

No one thinks they could survive!
Ah, but no! They're still alive.

Crispy, cruspy! Like a mouse,
Each is gnawing through his house.

And the baker's heard to say:
"Omigosh! They're getting away!"

Trick the sixth you just have read;
Trick the last is just ahead.

TRICK THE LAST

Max and Moritz, woe is you!
This trick will be the end of you!

Why is it that they must hack
Slits in every barley sack?

Look at that: it's Farmer Harley,
Shouldering a sack of barley.

Scarcely does he turn around
When the grain starts hitting ground.

And he stands, confused and blinking:
"What on earth!" he says; "it's shrinking!"

Ha! He discovers with a shout
Max and Moritz hiding out.

Rompf! He shoves the villains back
Into the bottom of his sack.

Max and Moritz now grow ill
As he takes them to the mill.

"Master Miller, my good man,
Grind this up as best you can!"

"Give it here!" He takes the jerks
And empties them into the works.

Rickarack! Rickarack!
The mill goes round, the rollers clack.

Here you see them one last time,
Cut apart and chopped up fine.

Soon they're eaten, every piece,

By the Master Miller's geese.

EPILOGUE

As the news went round the place,
Sorrow there was not a trace.
Widow Bolt spoke up benignly:
"Well, it had to happen finally!"
"Yes, oh yes," cried Master Swaim:
"Evil gives your life no aim!"
"Very true," said Pastor Lampel;
"This, once more, is an example!"
Said the baker, "That's the truth:
A sweet-tooth is a curse forsooth!"
Even goodly Uncle Fritz
Said, "That's what comes to wicked wits!"
The honest farmer said, said he:
"Guess that don't mean much to me!"
In short, each villager and farmer
Joined in one ecstatic murmur:
"Thanks be to God! From off our backs
Moritz is gone, and so is Max!"

Ice-Peter

A FUNNY
PICTURE-STORY

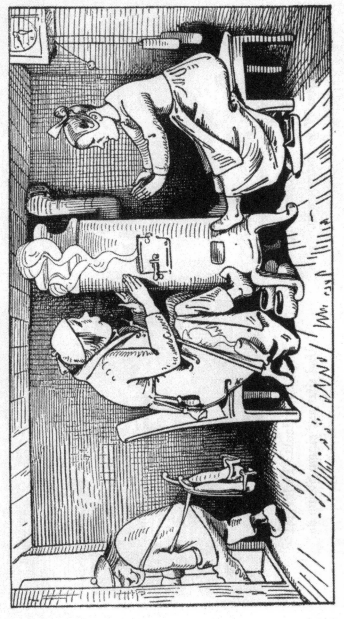

Way back in '12, the winds blew high,
The firewood was in short supply;

We nestled round our stoves and grates—
Except for Peter with his skates.

His uncle, the warden, warned and cried:
"It's much too cold to be outside!"

Outside, how strange it was to see:
The crows fell lifeless from the tree.

But Peter thinks: "I'll be all right,"
And sits to put his skates on tight.

And on the pathway there appears
A rabbit frozen by its ears.

63

The stuff is old, the need is great;
He rips them free and stands up straight.

Now Peter wants to stand and go;
His pants prefer the status quo.

The cap he loses is the price
Of crawling from the pool of ice.

Oh dear, I always feared the worst:
He skates into a hole head first.

Though small at first, upon his nose
A spike appears and quickly grows.

And soon the spikes are large as life
And sharp as any butcher's knife.

You ask me, What's that strange design?
Why, that's a frozen porcupine!

More and more the spikes appear;
The nasal spike becomes a spear.

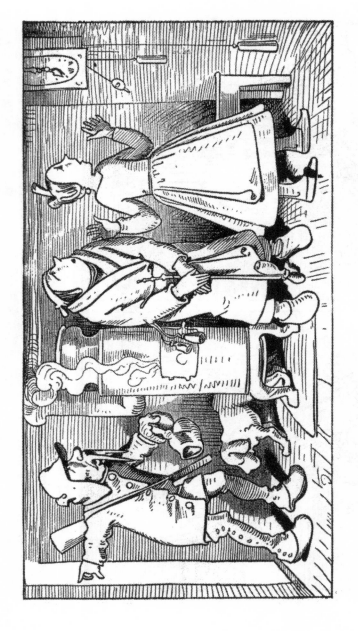

His parents watch the clock and wait:
"Oh, what is keeping him so late?"

His uncle comes inside and roars:
"The fool is wandering out of doors!"

Already, with an anxious glance,
They glimpse a shred of Peter's pants.

Bearing an ax and silent woe,
They search for Peter in the snow.

But then their sorrow was much greater
When they saw Peter not much later.

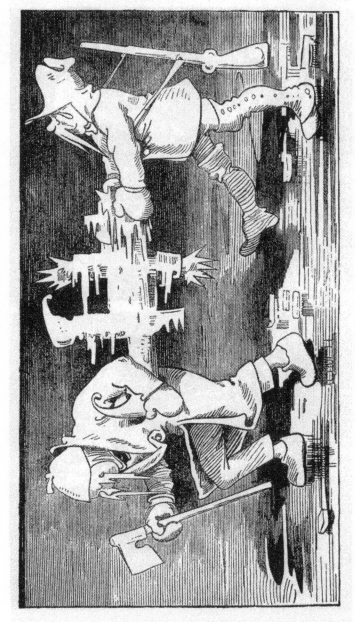

They carry him home with tears and sighs,
The teardrops freezing in their eyes.

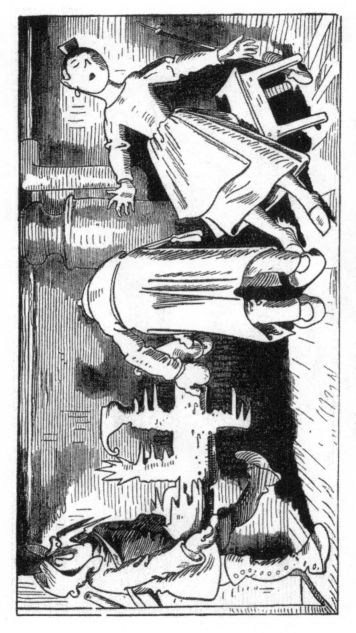

With care they let down Peter's members
Beside the stove to feel the embers

Hooray! The gladness is profuse:
The water runs, the ice comes loose.

But oh, look now! All hope is fled!
The boy entire runs out like lead.

And here into a pot is drained
The last of Peter that remained.

Yes, in this simple stoneware vessel
The last preserves of Peter nestle,

Who, after he at first was hard,
Later on got soft like lard.

Diogenes

AND THE
BAD BOYS OF
CORINTH

A barrel's rim to shade his eyes,
Diogenes in slumber lies.

A youthful roustabout who spied him
Calls to a friend to come beside him.

And now the ill-instructed boys
Start knocking, just to make some noise.

Diogenes peeps out to say,
"What's all this knocking anyway?"

The one with the cap on now comes back
Armed with a squirtgun for attack.

Straight through the bung, a forceful jet.
Diogenes gets soaking wet.

Just as Diogenes is yearning
To sleep, the ruffians are returning.

They roll the cask along with ease.
"Stop, stop!" cries out Diogenes.

But as they clasp the barrel,
They do not grasp their peril.

Two nails are partially exposed
And catch the villains by their clothes.

The miscreants are wailing,
Their arms and legs are flailing.

But tears and cries won't help them. No:
Under the barrel they must go.

Two rogues of Corinth: look at that!
Rolled out like cookies, broad and flat.

But Diogenes the Wise crept back under cover
And said, "Well, one thing leads to another!"

FROM
Critique of the Heart

"SHE WAS A FLOWERET GAY AND FINE..."

She was a floweret gay and fine,
Full-blooming in the sweet sunshine.
He was a youthful butterfly
Who loved the flower and stayed close by.

Sometimes, with a great buzzing sound,
A bee would bumble all around.
And sometimes—kribblekrab—the beetles
Crept up and down the fragile petals.

To see such things, oh what a dart
Went through the butterfly's young heart!

These shocking scenes were all surpassed,
However, by what happened last:
A dumb old donkey gulped down whole
The plant that so entranced his soul.

THE GIFT

Three aunts sat down with wrinkled brow.
The first said: "Girls, we had better
Decide about Sophie's birthday now.
So what are we going to get her?"

The second aunt spoke swift and keen:
"Why, I've got a certain winner:
A simple dress in a shade of green
That will cause her to lose her dinner."

"Great!" said the third, "And for extra offense,
Big ruffles in purple and tan!
I'm sure she'll be madder than three wet hens,
And must thank us as best she can."

THE FOX AND THE FARMER

The fox was breathing the forest air.
The farmer sent him a letter there:
"Please do come by! All is forgiven;
There is no need for getting even.
The cock, the hens and all the geese
Will greet you with the kiss of peace.
And so: when should we have the party?
                    Yours in true friendship,
                    Christian Hardy"
The fox wrote back in goose's blood:
"Doesn't look good:
My wife just had another brood!
I send, as always, my highest regard.
                    Your friend in the cave,
                    Renard"

THE HUMORIST

Stuck fast in birdlime on his tree,
The bird flaps hard, but can't get free.
A big black cat comes creeping low;
His claws are sharp, his eyes aglow.
On up the tree and ever higher,
The murderous beast approaches nigher.
The bird thinks: "Well, since that is that—
I must be eaten by the cat—
I will not let a moment go,
I'll practice all the trills I know
And whistle merrily, undeterred."
I call that humor in a bird.

Wilhelm Busch
(1832-1908)

Wilhelm Busch was born in Wiedensahl, near Hannover, Germany, in 1832. He first learned drawing from his uncle and was proficient by age 13. His father wanted him to be a machinist, and Busch himself aspired to be a great painter like Rembrandt. His style as a comic illustrator evolved while he was a young man living in Munich and contributing to a humor magazine called "Flying Pages" (*Fliegende Blätter*).

Max und Moritz (1865) was Busch's first major work, and he never duplicated its success, although he continued to produce his "picture-stories" (*Bildergeschichten*) till 1883.

He was even less lucky in love. For two weeks in 1864 he dated a young woman in Wolfenbüttel (we don't know her name), but he didn't propose marriage then because he couldn't support a wife. When he asked after her again some years later, she had married. Busch never did. (This experience may have inspired the poem, "She was a floweret gay and fine," included here on page 89.)

In later years, Busch became more and more of a hermit, rolling his own cigarettes, 40 a day. He died in 1908, leaving a creative legacy that includes sculpture and poetry as well as cartoons—and paintings: he was a good painter too. Still, we remember him not because he took his place beside the Flemish master painters of old, but because he took his place beside the American master comic-strip artists of the future. And as comic strips, now a global art form, continue to evolve, Wilhelm Busch still keeps pace with the best in the field, fresh as tomorrow and twice as funny.

Andy Gaus, *Translator*

Andy Gaus is the author of *The Unvarnished New Testament*, a complete translation from the Greek, and a collection of translations from the German of Rainer Maria Rilke entitled *Requiem for a Woman*. A composer and lyricist as well as a translator, Andy has written songs and scores for revues, musicals and operas produced in Boston, where he makes his home.

CPSIA information can be obtained
at www.ICGtesting.com
Printed in the USA
BVHW081919221119
564529BV00002B/246/P